Escape from Stupid

Poetry, Vignette & Nonfiction
by
Skeeter Wilson

To my writers group in Alaska, the Afterthoughts, and Dave Onofrychuk, who saved me from my life of poetry, vignettes, and nonfiction and put me on the higher path of fiction.

And to life. It has been worth it for the most part.

CONTENTS

Poetry & Vignette   1

Africa: Nonfiction   19

America: Nonfiction   32

Alaska: Nonfiction   41

FORWARD

I grew up in Kenya, the son of American missionaries, and came to America when I was nineteen. In my early adult life, I lived in Tennessee, Georgia, and Washington State. It was a time of cultural adjustment, marriage, children, and divorce. During my separation and divorce, I moved to Alaska, and I lived and worked there for ten years.

Escape from Stupid is a written scrapbook of those years composed of poetry, vignettes, and nonfiction.

Now, I am remarried, happily, writing fiction, and at peace.

POETRY AND VIGNETTE

Independence Day
Sticks and clubs crack hard
on skins of hollowed Percussion.
They Drone on and on,
calling out to Africa's soils.

A furious Harmony of twisting
arms, legs, skins, vivid colors
flaunts shields and spears wielded
before masks of birds, monkeys, demons, beasts.

The bronze Chorus, kissed by the sun's millennia,
beats and slices the air with their instruments,
whose jagged edges not so long ago
urged this day along by blood-soaked sinew.

Screams and howls and roars declare in Unison
Uhuru! Independence Day!

Her Majesty's pith helmets
in rows of decadent Descant,
silenced to silence
in colonial power's fading displays.

I, the audience, sat alone to it all.
I saw what could only be seen without words.
I was there, yes I, as one kissed neither by the sun
nor suckled by royal lineage.

I too belonged to that blood-soaked soil,
given to me by birth,
in the aftermath of which, I saw it all.
I, yes, I alone witnessed that Ensemble day.

I Hummed and tapped in quiet consent.
I clapped for joy, I cried in fear,
for I knew not for what
or whom the next Song might be.

I did not run. I stood. I roared.

You watch the edited story sitting on your
couch. You eat buttered popcorn as a
double faces a vicious, choreographed charge.

You see that mange-ridden beast lying in stale feces while
little ones giggle and stare and laugh, bravely prodding their
smudges on the glass.

You ride the big safari over tire-riddled fields. You see the
guaranteed prides, which only money can buy, amidst
caviar and brandied teas.

You must know more about lions
than I could ever hope to know.

But I have walked those savannahs. No
iron bars or warning labels, no scripts,
no edits, no stunt doubles, no second takes.

Just once, I chose a rare path, and spelled
so by the beauty of the morning, I
missed their dusted impressions, and

I stumbled upon both royal beast and cubs and
surprised both them and me. They snarled their
pleasure at such an unexpected feast.

I did what I did. Perhaps
by instinct, but not skill.

I did not run. I stood. I roared.

I listened to my own, unexpected, primeval, nasty

human roar. The lions turned on cue and fled. I stood,
I shook, then on wobbled legs, I went the other way.

I know more about lions, than you could ever hope to know.

The Hunter and the Little One

"Will the hunter's feast be ready soon?" her young voice asked plaintively of the figure stooping over the cooking fire.

The array of aromatics had captivated her into maddening fits of hunger.

"Little one, the meal begins after the sun finds rest behind that mountain." The rasp in his voice was belied by the amusement in his eyes as he nodded in the direction of Africa's afternoon glow.

His hands deftly turned the spit over the flames of the cooking fire. With each rotation, fresh wafts of delectable essence exploded through the tiny village.

She ran through the village to the edge of the rainforest and stopped, mesmerized by new respect for the mountain soaring resolutely over her immense world. She stood oblivious to the bustle of communal life behind her and to the evening chores her mother implored of her.

Hue-laden rays brushed shades of crimson on the mist that perpetually rose above the forest canopy.

She sat.

She stood.

She sat and stood.

She hesitated then scampered back to his side.

"Does the hunter know the sun rests for the little one first?"

"Little one, I need a taster to see if the game is ready for the village feast."

She smiled her triumph.

I Was Born Beneath the Shadows

of the mountain's fading, blue, distant memory,
a broken line beyond the yawn of
Africa's plains, paled and dusted by
whirling wisps dangling in the air,

a jagged, single-sided edge
above a forbidden valley of
rumor and speculation,
a rusted wing in stillborn flight.

Fading rays paint
color on top of color in
a feverish flurry until a deep purple
bids the day goodbye.

Thousands of insects tune their
pitch for a grand finale. They
cheer the coal black that then
cloaks the mountain from the sky.

There are claims now of chains that
clasp the hollow hill,
which once was a playing field
of man and boys and beast, and
that the yawn is full of hewn logs
that tin now sap the view of memories
that wander in the past.

And the cloak is not as black,
and the music not so strong,
but a mist still rises above the mountain.

And I am born again beneath its shadow.

path

feet
     blissful
     lamenting
pressed
     sage
     engraved
in history
     irrefutable
     unrequited
     expatiating

Unveiling

I sit by the water rippling wide across rocks,
each stone polished smooth by monsoons,

relentless water grinding Africa into submission
beneath its seasons. The sun, still partially

submerged behind misty hills, sends
shafts of muted light through the trees.

Early hues of cherry and ginger dance in
the clouds and on the painted mist rising

on the breath of the morning air. Thin blades
of light unveil treasures on the forest floor: dew

masquerading as diamonds, shattering each blade
into the full spectrum, dew dazzling on leaves

and flowers, dew dancing on the myriad webs
engineered by builders dangling from unknowable

heights. I sit in the shadow of the fading night,
watching. Darkness pushes against light but yields

to the sun. I sit, veiled in Africa's forests, until
I am discovered by the light as I sit by the water

rippling wide across rocks.

Comfort

So I will slip out of comfort,
no longer comfortable,
and thread the thin waves of air
and bursts of cloud and light and stars
in search of the uneasy and unknowable,

where I will break my alabaster jar upon
the rocks and waste my memories to the
wind and dirt and decay in search of
where hands have not defined the space
and contemplate comfort a different way.

She Tied Me Up Good

I knowed once'st a woman down Tennessee way.
She charmed up my love the sweet Southern way.
She tied me up good on da wedding day.

I had me a wife; ya, she bore us two sons.
In da red Georgia clay, we reared up two sons.
We raised 'em on Jesus, green okra, an' guns.

I till'd up the soil an' planted red beans,
sweet corn an' peppas an' green string beans.
Pulled up dem taters, best ever seens.

I fetched me a dog, a goat, an' some hens,
Rhode Islan' roosta' an' fryers an' hens.
We ate gravy on grits an' eggs from dem pens.

Wit' toil an' labor I built us a home.
We moved an' we shifted, but I kept us a home.
The boys became men an' then left us alone.

I knowed once't a woman down Tennessee way.
She packed up an' left me an' went on her way.
She tied me up good; nuttin' more ta say.

The Planter Box

August breathed its flames
upon my window, mocking
my Thoreau impression, planted
to ensure my escape—along
with my morning coffee—and
to remind me
it was not so long ago

April captured first my eyes,
and I responded
to its fragrant pleasures and
placed tender roots
in boxes upon the sill to
populate the moments
until the iron bars of

December begin their vigil
and I hide behind blinds
from the frozen fingers
that will crush the tender roots
until my anniversary day,
when early in each

March, I peer out to see
if my frozen pond is
ready for a new beginning or if
the swan might return or if
I can still believe or
love again.

Super bowl

This running game sucks. Why don't they pass the fucking
football? Come on now. Is that pizza done yet? That was a catch—
what is wrong with them? —that was a fucking great catch. Why
don't they find younger refs who can actually see the game? They
should challenge that call. Fumble my ass. Dammit, these stuffed
mushrooms are great. What did you put in these things? Hey, did
you all see that movie, you know, the one about the dreams, sort of
manipulating people through dreams? Oh my god, that was a
messed up movie. Who was that actor, the boy child, Leonard
Decaffeinated? Yeah, I'm getting another rum and Coke. So you
want just a shot of JD? Shut up! I missed the touchdown. FUCK.
What happened? Everyone is talking during the game and watching
the commercials—this is gay. Fuck, that girl is hot. She can't hear
me. Yeah, I know she's married, but she's still hot. I didn't say I
wanted to do her, did I? No more ice. How did we run out of ice, it
isn't even half time yet? Hey, I'm not complaining, man. I'm just
pointing out the facts. This is your party—deal with it. Darth Vader
commercial? No, I didn't see the cute little Darth-Vader-in-a-
Volkswagen commercial. What are we, a bunch of Nazi lovers
now? Radish cheese? Who eats radish cheese? No, the Coke is cold
enough, thanks. Yep, the crab dip is great. You made it? Oh my
god, I'm poisoned! Hey, I'm just kidding. You want to get coffee
sometime? No, I'm not asking you out on a date, for god's sake.
You're my friend's wife. You're just a smoking hot woman, and I
wanted to know if you want to go get coffee sometime. What? I
know I'm a guest. I haven't made a mess, have I? Yes, I have been
talking, but so has everyone else. I don't know how much I've had
to drink—I'm not counting. This is a party—this is the biggest
party day of the year—and I can't have a little fun? No, I didn't
touch your wife. I didn't insult you. It's halftime—let me just see
the halftime show, and I'll behave myself. Good fuck'n grief, I'm
not hurting anybody, am I? Black Eyed Piss? Oh my god, look at
the bundles of joy on that woman. Who gives a fuck if she can

sing, the question is can she fuck as good as she looks? Okay, I won't talk about her tits. I'll just look and make comparisons. Are the Chargers winning? Oh fuck, I know they aren't playing. My words are just getting jumbled up a little. This is a party, man. Be cool. FUCK NO. What the hell are you doing? You can't make me leave, man. I haven't done anything. Who did I insult? Oh fuck all of you. I'm leaving then. You all are a bunch of fucked up queers. This is America, man. What the fuck is wrong with all of you? Hey, man, I need to use the john first. You know, I need to take a whiz, man. Really. Don't make me leave before I take a whiz. That isn't cool, man. Just this one thing, and then I'll go, I promise. But damn, your wife looks really hot, man. She has a smoking ass. I would love to tap—oh fuck, don't hit me. Shit.

"You're Tired of this Old World at Last"

with T. L. O'Hara

Tired of this old world at last, I wilt.
Cut. Tossed among the leaves of grass
smoldering on the shit pile. Compost.
Empty of living, of line, of remorse.

On gathering day, something fell within me,
and I made no pretense to my collectors.
Bundled with the rest of the dead and dying, they
carted me away as discard, as still living refuse.

Mingled with the scattered sinews of my remains
and the incense this rot provides, life bursts
from the heaped decay—accounts now levied on
those who pinched their nose at my befouled demise.

And had they known—if had they known—what
now, if not nothing, would be the single difference?
Would the weathering of experience and time have
dealt more temperance upon this stem, these roots?

Alas, no more can one stifle death through will
than will their own entombed embers to life.
Free will? Bah! What coddled farce played on
the awakenings and slumberings of the soil.

And so, I sleep, with no misplaced remorse. Ashes
to ashes. Dust to dust. And the rest is silence.
When the scythe strikes, worry not where or why
your petals lie: you are returning; you have returned.

Hey Diddle Cliché

Why cry o'er the cow
who kicked the bucket,
which spilt the milk,
when you screamed as

you sat on the needle that
your mother lost in the hay?
Your voice shocked the flock

who pecked the blackberries,
which grow by the cliff,
who feathered together and
whirred off to silver-lined clouds,

and the cow went lickety-split.

Terminal

Growing old is terminal, yet
my mind refuses to give up hope that
one day there may be a cure.

Growing old is filled with memories that
do not relinquish their hold
and sap youth from the veins.

Growing old is when idealism dies and
the noble thoughts of tomorrow end in
silent, forbidden dreams.

Growing old is understanding, finally, that
the imagination of youth is nothing but
the fear of growing old.

Speak

Only one can be free
    whose debtors have been freed.

Only one can take charge
    who will not take the lead.

Only one can confront tears
    who has bitterly learned to weep.

Only one can learn to give
    who has nothing left to keep.

Only one can speak of cost
    who has tasted once the hell of it.

Only one can speak of death
    who has died and lived to tell of it.

AFRICA: NONFICTION

Father

I breathed deeply, tasting the salty ocean air. I felt the rush of water gently tugging at my feet, inching me away from shore. The water went slack before the next wave urged me back to the white sand beach in Mombasa.

I had never learned to swim, because there are no waters deep enough for swimming in the African rainforests where I grew up. I was careful to stay waist-deep, knowing something of the riptides of African beaches. My friends had disappeared down the beach in search of perfect cowry shells. I watched the surf breaking on the coral reefs and the emerald-green ocean beyond.

Every year, my friend Dean had tried to persuade me to go to the coast with his family for their annual vacation. Finally, I had agreed. I was eighteen years old, and I had wanted to visit Africa's coastline at least once before leaving for America after graduating boarding school. And other than the fact my parents had decided to come on vacation with me, it had been a perfect trip. I felt a happy discontent.

Then I was tumbling underwater.

A churning current had dragged me from the shoreline. I tried to stand, but there was nothing to stand on. In a jolt of fear, I opened my eyes, and sandy, brackish water stung me to blindness; salty water seared my lungs. I flailed my arms and legs desperately. I struggled to the surface and found a brief reprieve. I choked and screamed, and the water was cleared from my lungs. I gasped for air and glimpsed my father standing on the beach watching me. Then a surge of undertow pulled me violently back under, and I tumbled and scraped along the sea bottom. But the glimpse of my father had given me a flicker of hope. He was a lifeguard once; he would save me.

The undertow scraped my body along jagged ocean rocks then pushed me down into a deep hole of calm water. I realize I was in what was a tidal pool at low tide. For a moment, the rushing water above me slowed. My lungs were bursting with the need for air, and I pushed hard against the bottom and shot up toward the surface, pulled slightly shoreward by the crest of a wave. At the surface, I coughed water and managed a few gasps of air, screaming again for help. Then I was twisted and plunged back into the water just as I caught another glimpse of my father, still standing on the beach watching me, unmoved.

The tyrannical undertow flung me back to the bottom, and this time, I grabbed on to one of the jagged rocks large enough to anchor me. The water tore past me, prying at my grip, trying to pull me away from Africa. Then the water slackened again, and I pushed myself desperately back to the surface. A welcome wave again took me a small distance closer to the shore, and I looked toward the beach and screamed to the diminishing figure standing there.

I had learned to hold my breath by now each time I was slammed again onto the rocks below, and I was gulping more air during my brief moments the surface. I held on to the bottom during each rip out to sea and pushed myself back to the surface to try to catch the next wave toward shore. The task seemed impossible, but I felt a slight progress back to land. I was getting weaker, and on the beach stood the solitary figure of the man who was called my father.

At what felt like the far side of eternity, I found myself back on the beach, bent over and vomiting. Then I felt a crushing blow from an open palm on my back. I turned to avoid another blow and looked into the angry eyes of my father.

"You stupid, good-for-nothing idiot! That was a dumb stunt out there, pretending to drown. Didn't you learn about the boy who cried wolf?

Next time, when you're really in trouble, no one's going to help you."

I briefly stared at the man biology had used to make me, and I felt a great sigh as I realized what my soul had always known, that this man was never my father.

African Killer Bees

One of the first things I think of when I think of my mother is bees. Not just any bees—African killer bees.

My mother and I and my four siblings were having a picnic under the acacia trees near Lake Navasha, not far from our home in Kenya, when killer bees swarmed and attacked. My mother took all five of us and buried our faces in her breasts to protect us.

We children only suffered a few stings, but my mother's face was filled with swollen, red welts, and when the bees moved on, she barely made it to the hospital in time.

She could have died, but she was willing to give her life for her children.

I was too young to remember the bees. However, my older siblings rolled their eyes every time my mother told this story. They do not remember it this way.

They do not remember a swarm of bees, though she was stung a few times. And she did go to the hospital but only the next day and only then as a precaution because she insisted she was so near death's door.

I have many memories of such stories, but I never knew if any of what my mother told me was true.

She told me how much I should appreciate my father, how lucky I was to have such a wonderful man who had dedicated his life to helping Africans who needed to better their lives.

My mother never explained why my famous father abused his children. She only told me I should be grateful.

She never told me about her childhood.

I never knew my mother, not really. She could not have realized how hard it was to listen to her stories, not knowing what, if anything, existed outside of her imagination.

If my mother had told me about her childhood, I would have doubted more than I believed. But I sometimes wonder if her childhood might go some distance toward illuminating the stranger I knew as my mother.

Escape from Stupid

There are many labels that might have been tried out on me if I
had grown up in the United States: slightly autistic, inattentive
hypoactive, chronic depressive, bipolar, and a host of others.

Fortunately or not, growing up and attending boarding school,
there was only one label for me: stupid. Stupid is a label one does
not live around when growing up in a small, cloistered town in the
African rainforests. I even accepted, when I was being sexually
abused by my father, that I deserved it simply because I was stupid.

My one escape from stupid was poetry.

What I could never bring myself to express, I found a way to
express in poetry. Darkness, brooding, anger, and pain filled page
after page. Sometimes, I wrote simple verses, and other times,
entire notebooks were filled with epic-style stanzas made of
couplets and quatrains.

Raw, untrained, and often hidden from my understanding, my
writing began with poetry.

I still did not dispute the stupid label. I assumed the mass of
questions in my head were a part of the madness of my stupidity.
My label seemed well deserved when I stared at jumbles of letters
on paper, emptily entertained by the rush of thoughts in my mind.

Then as I crept into my teenage years, my poetry began to
give way to prose, and I began to feel I was not the idiot I always
seemed. Though the first teacher to test my IQ decided I had
somehow fluked the test, as my score placed my intelligence in the
top half percentile.

Much of my formal education was wasted. When others were
learning how to spell, I was struggling to get the letters simply to sit
still on the page. I never outgrew the dyslexia entirely, but I learned
to read books despite. I learned if I did not look directly at the
words, I could comprehend the sentences and the paragraphs. But
reading has always remained hard work for me, and though I have
always loved to read, I have always hated reading.

As my prose writing grew, I began to write analytical think

pieces. I explored everything through my pen. Philosophy, religion and politics took cyclical turns being deconstructed, revised, and reconstituted on the page. But my writing remained for my own personal freedom. Even after my mind began to put things in order, even after I found a voice and a way to make a place for myself in the world, there was never a safer place for me.

As the world became less dark and less confusing, and when joys like my sons came into my life, there was a decided shift in my writing. I began to watch people around me and began to write short nonfiction and vignettes based on people I met.

Some of my prose found its way to the public.

One piece I wrote on how to build a composting toilet made its way into a small magazine. A short vignette I wrote about my first visit to Alaska ended up in a tourist brochure. A couple of essays I wrote concerning theology became part of an anthology of religious issues.

But life got in the way of my pen. I had children to raise, a dog to annoy, employees to look after, and customers to attend to.

Years were spent keeping the candle lit at both ends. Work evolved into eighty, ninety, and sometimes one hundred hours a week. And one day, the flames at either end of the candle met, and I crashed. I mentally, physically, and emotionally imploded into a massive ball of clinical depression. Terror, chaos, and long forgotten memories strove to destroy the small island of sanity that separated me from the chaos that had defined my childhood.

But I built a new island. I built it with writing. Writing remains the safe place I can go in the chaos.

I am writing poetry again, but it is no longer so dark. I am writing nonfiction again, but it is no longer so hopeless, because I am not so hopeless. In the improbable course of time, the improbable has happened—a wife whom I love and am capable of loving—and I have stumbled across that illusive thing called happiness.

My writing has been and remains more than poetry or prose. My writing is my escape, and more, it is my sanity.

My Name is Rungu

A lone figure strode toward me in the distance. An occasional puff of dust whirled behind him as he stepped between jagged volcanic rocks in the desert sand. His progress was slow.

Northern Kenya is not kind to travelers. The burning sand can sear through sandals as if they do not exist, while rocks can cut the leather soles to shreds, and thorns from the brush hook their way into the skin, leaving dangerous wounds.

Even a small overturned stone might reveal a deadly scorpion beneath its shadow, and there are precious few places to escape the hellish heat of midday. Sane people do not travel in the heat, preferring the shade of the occasional large rock while waiting for the day to cool before resuming their journey.

And I wanted no visitors on that bittersweet day. It was my private farewell to Kenya, to Africa.

Soon I would be heading to America. My nineteen years in Kenya since my birth were ending. I was a participant in a decades-long procession of foreign children in Africa who, upon reaching adulthood, are obligated to leave the land and people of their birth and return to the land of their parents' citizenship. I had come to this little piece of desert, my last trip to a place that had stolen my heart, and my intention was to spend a week staring into the African sky, weeping silently.

But the week had not gone as planned.

I was staying at a station in the home of friends who had gone to a town that was a three-day drive away. The only other resident of the station lay drenched in sweat, fighting an awful case of malaria.

Then two men arrived with word that a water hole had run dry and a desperate band of Rendille nomads were in danger of losing their lives if they did not receive food and water soon. So, my seclusion was interrupted, because I was the only person available to drive the needed supplies to the nomads.

I spent a grueling day and a half of nonstop driving with my two guides as I slowly maneuvered the Land Rover through roadless lava beds toward a vague destination.

As the sun bombarded its heat into the dark green vehicle, we stopped again and again to repair a damaged tire or tailpipe or to refill the gas tank from jerricans. The desert rocks, like jagged spikes, made the tire repairs an almost futile task, and we were running out of gas and uncertain how much longer our journey would be.

The sun and the growing desperation of our own situation drove us to continue.

As the day sank into the relief of a cool evening, the mosquitoes began their relentless task of assaulting every portion of our exposed skin. Eagerly drawn to our blood, they left in their wake the constant threat of malaria, and by night's end, even the scorching sun seemed welcome when compared with the miserable creatures.

We arrived amidst shouts and chants of welcome from some very desperate people. After unloading the vehicle, I sank into some shade, exhausted from the sleepless journey.

I was quickly roused by one of the guides who informed me a nomad elder had been bitten by a snake and was losing consciousness. Death was certain if he did not get help soon. The nearest usable airstrip was a day's drive away. We quickly set up a mobile radio and called to arrange to meet a plane carrying a nurse at the remote airstrip the next morning.

We loaded the moaning elder into the Land Rover and drove off in the heat of the day in search of the airstrip. As the tires bumped over each rock, the motion was echoed by a moan from the miserable invalid, but time would not allow for comfort to be a consideration.

Two sleepless nights and three sunbaked days brought time to a delirious standstill.

Somewhere out of that eternity, the airstrip appeared. A plane waited with figures waving us to them. Sapped of all strength, my two guides and I struggled to shift the almost lifeless body from

our vehicle to the floor of the small single engine craft. Virtually
without words, nurse, patient, and pilot were racing down the
bumpy path and into the sky, leaving us alone and with little idea of
the success of our torturous journey.

Simple survival bid us on. We had to reach my guides' own
nomadic village by nightfall, or our lives, too, would be in danger.

Through the delirious day, we were mocked by an endless line
of mirages; trees and water danced in the sand and rocks that lay
before us. As evening approached, we nearly drove past the village,
thinking it was only another mirage.

At last the Land Rover wandered into the village to shouts of
joy as my guides were greeted by their relatives.

Finally, in the safety of the village, it took little time for me to
be found stretched out on my bedroll, my first chance for sleep in
almost four days. I found a fire and turned my back to it and tried
to drown out the voices and chanting that surrounded its embers.
But just as my exhaustion began to melt into a fitful sleep, I was
shaken awake. A young man informed me the elders wanted me to
sit with them in the elders circle.

Every aching part of me wanted to scream a desperate No!
But saying no to the elders is not among the options available to a
visitor. Soon I was sitting in a circle of men who looked as ancient
as the land itself. They began to ask me questions and requested
accounts of our journey from my guides.

Barely knowing a word of Rendille, I spoke my Swahili
through a translator, who also kept me informed of the various
conversations.

Slowly, a ceremonial gourd was being passed around so each
member of the circle could sip its contents. Along with the gourd
was passed a ceremonial club of honor, a *rungu*.

It is against Rendille custom to allow a nontribal person to sit
in the circle of elders, but there I sat, and it is considered a curse
for a nontribal person to drink from the ceremonial gourd, but it
was slowly being passed toward me. I squirmed with growing
discomfort. A wrong decision to drink or pass the gourd could be

dangerous, even fatal.

The gourd arrived in the hands of the silent but kindly gray-headed man next to me. I watched as he tipped the contents toward his mouth and drank deeply. Then he passed the gourd to me and, sensing my discomfort, motioned for me to drink.

I slowly tilted the gourd to my mouth. I closed my eyes and drank the concoction of coal blackened curdled milk, cow blood, and human urine, knowing any signs of disgust would earn me a most cruel disgrace. The raw, putrid effect in my throat left me speechless and silently gasping for air. But I managed to pass the gourd and the *rungu* to the next circle member in as solemn and dignified a manner as possible.

The elders talked of the stars, their gods and mine, the earth, and the cruel nature of life. They talked of their fellow elder, who was the miserable snakebite victim my guides and I had taken to the airstrip; they laughed at the thought him flying in a large bird. They asked me about the world beyond their own. And they shook their heads in bewilderment that I was soon leaving to another land for good.

Late into the night, they agreed that I looked tired and ready for rest, and I was mercifully allowed to return to my bedroll. I slept deeply and was woken early and was given a cheerful send-off for my half-day drive back to the station where the whole journey had begun.

The morning after I returned to the station, I watched the lone figure continue his way toward me. It was my last day at the station, and I had been sitting under the shade of a rock and savoring that small corner of God's earth.

I watched the figure, disgusted at the possible interruption and hoping he would soon see me and respectfully change his course. But as he came closer, the features of his face became increasingly clear, and I began to suspect he was the elder who sat next to me in the elders circle. It was. And I began to worry about what I could have done to cause an elder to walk so many miles through such a cruel desert in the middle of the day.

The elder approached me breathing easily, exhibiting the strength of a man born to the region. In his hand, he held the *rungu*. He handed the club to me and said, "We honor you. We declare you to be a man. We declare you to be one with us. We now call you Rungu. We ask that one day you return to us." Then in a gesture of deep respect, he pounded a fist once against his chest and slowly opened his palm over his heart. Then he turned and walked back into the desert.

When he had gone, I looked at the *rungu* and wondered at my passage into manhood by a people I truly loved and who, in many ways, still lived in the Iron Age, and I wondered what meaning my manhood could have in the America I was soon to be exiled to.

A week after that solemn day, I sat aboard a jet as it lifted off. With one hand touching the *rungu* in my carry-on, I pounded my fist once against my chest and slowly opened my palm over my heart as I watched Kenya, my Africa, fall away beneath me.

Visiting Kenya After Thirty Years

In spite of some changes, it remains very much the same.

Animals still roam the plains, perhaps not as many, but the abundance is still breathtaking. The hills still rise above the plains in majestic wonder.

Cars still play roulette at maddening speeds on narrow ribbons of broken road, and pedestrians still wander between the chasing cars with detached disinterest. *Matatus* still brim while the drivers' assistants stand on the precarious outside edge of traffic urging new travelers into the fracas.

Mendazies still taste like heaven's manna dipped in Kenyan chai. The savor of *irio*, *nyma choma*, and stews still satisfy the soul.

There is the abject poverty of millions, detached from their tribal homelands, bursting out of the cities and onto the roadsides, setting up squatters huts in the fields and right-of-ways, and spilling into the vast plains of Africa. Displacement seems a choking crises without a resolution.

From this crisis has grown the "apartheid of chains," as my friends in my hometown of Kijabe described it. Those with deeper pockets have built fortresses of steel and wire and live in "mooted castles" removing themselves from those who would beg, steal, maim, or kill to survive.

On one hand, I see a partnership between the *mKenya* (Kenyans) and the missionaries and other *mzalendo* (noncitizens). They have formed a bond and communication such as I never saw before. But on the other hand, the deceptions of fear are driving them apart and threaten the new alliance.

I have seen disappointment etched on the faces of those who call themselves *wanainchi* (the people or citizens of the land) because the *wazungu* (white people) have allowed fear to tear a chasm between themselves and the Kenyans who they call their brethren. The *wanainchi* speak of the joy of the salvation that the strange *wazungu* preach, but they look with sad eyes at the rift that now separates them. "Why," one Kenyan Bible teacher asked me, "do we find them trusting in fences rather than God?"

But I wonder at the depth of forgiveness. "After all," the *wanainchi* say, "we cannot forget that like us, the *wazungu* are frail human beings too." I find this type of forgiveness utterly amazing.

I feel the despair as indicated by the number of hand written addresses stuffed in my pockets. While I am glad to have the contacts, it is their reasons that sadden me. Young and old, educated and uneducated, they all want to go America. They want an inside track to a green card. They want their life energy to be expended, not in their home, but in the epic they imagine America to be. I mourn their despair, their absence of confidence, their raw fear. Their hope is not gone, but it is very thin.

The razor edge of hope is political. Beaming with pride to a man, they described to me their first "open, free, and fair" election. A fragile belief is welling up that at last is the end of a dictatorial reign of corruption and there is now the presence of an open and critical press. All this despite the breaking of a major campaign promise before the end of the first year.

I wonder to myself if this truly is a new political era for Kenya, as my friends believe. Or if it is a cruel setup for a crushing disappointment. Either way, right now, in a single moment of time, it is clear that this new president has as much political capitol as any leader could ask for. If he has the courage and strength to be a president for the people and not his party, he will go down in the nation's history as an icon.

In the end, my joy is the connection of souls, the invitations to homes, the calls to return, the statements that I was never a real *wazungu* and I belong in the *shambas* of Africa with those mended of the same heart. My joy is the understanding and common ideas, which almost thirty years of absence were unable to erase.

AMERICA: NONFICTION

Coming to America

The sign read Restroom. I suppose I was too tired to guess this was a colloquial euphemism deeply embedded in the American lexicon. My African English was full of euphemisms, but I was exhausted. I was not thinking in euphemisms.

It had taken me nearly fifty hours with endless layovers to fly from my home in Kenya to my home to be in America. I had no idea one could be so exhausted from nothing but sitting.

I sludged through the airport terminal following the signs that read Baggage Claim. I vaguely wondered why I needed to claim my own bags.

But then the Restroom signs appeared.

I really did not have time to rest, but I was impressed. Americans think of everything. They have rooms for resting in their airports. I could not resist the urge to check them out. So, I followed the signs.

There were two doors. One sign read Men, the other Women. Ah, Americans! No chance of hanky-panky in the airport because the men rest in one room and the women in another. I pushed open the door under the sign that read Men, expecting to see rows of lounge chairs filled with men resting from their travels.

But I was surprised, and slightly disappointed. Though, I did find some relief inside.

***

I was straddling him, my fingers digging deep into his neck, and I watched his eyes bulge and his face turn pink and then red as I restricted the blood flow to his brain. His name was Dorsey Kimball. And I was about to find out the man I was trying to kill was my new boss.

It was the first day of my first job in America. I began to realize the noisy factory machines had gone quiet and people were shouting and running toward me. I looked at Dorsey again and saw the terror in his eyes. I suddenly understood he was not trying to kill me, and I jumped off him and stood up.

"What is it that you have been doing to cause me to hurt you?" I said in my African English.

Dorsey gasped for air and stared at me in stunned disbelief. "Me? What did I do? You nearly killed me, you stupid fucking foreigner."

Hands grabbed and held me. Other hands helped Dorsey to his feet. Hands pushed me and Dorsey into the office of Bill, the plant manager.

And Bill seemed to understand what neither Dorsey nor I did.

Bill understood in my culture no person comes up to another from behind and taps them on the shoulder. He understood when Dorsey tapped me on the shoulder from behind, I thought I was under attack.

In Africa, things that come from behind unannounced are never good things.

"Skeeter, this is your new boss, Dorsey Kimball. You need to understand when people in America tap you on the shoulder from behind, it does not mean they are trying to kill you. Dorsey, this kid just arrived in America. You might want to approach him from the front until he gets used to living here."

I stared at Bill in disbelief. I will never get used to living here, I thought.

***

"Hey, Skeeter, how d'you get to work?"

"I walk."

"You walk? Your job's ten miles from your apartment. Why don't you drive?"

"It is not far to walk. I don't need a car."

"You foreigners do weird things. What way d'you walk?"

"I walk down Ninth Street."

"Are you stupid? That's the most violent street in town. Don't you listen to the news?"

"No."

"Those people on Ninth Street don't like white people. And we don't like them."

"I like them. They seem friendly."

"You're a fool then. They may act friendly, but they'll stab you in the back. Don't tell anyone around here that you like black people. You'll see burning crosses, and you'll end up in a body bag."

"What is a body bag?"

Tex

Tex was a man from another era. I only met him a few times because I lived in Africa, which was "too far to get to by horse."

Tex "hailed from Texas" but moved to Arizona shortly after my mother was born. He was a tall man, over six feet six inches, which for a man of his generation was "a hairsbreadth short of a giant."

I met him for the first time as a child when my parents, who were missionaries in Kenya, brought us briefly to America to visit family.

We were sitting on the porch with my grandmother, a short spitfire of a woman, jabbering on and on—excited to see my mother and her grandchildren after so many years. I had endured several sloppy kisses on my face and neck and thereafter kept my distance to ward off further assaults.

That was when I saw the cowboy. Well, he looked like one to me. He was riding up to the ranch house on a huge horse that was chestnut colored on its front quarters and spotted white and chestnut on its hind.

The cowboy was also a giant. He stepped off the horse like it was a miniature pony. He wore a dusty, tan ten-gallon hat and boots with silver tips and spurs. And a giant belt buckle.

I saw a lot of that belt buckle. No, not on my backside, fortunately—though my mother used to say she had scars from that same buckle. I saw it, more than anything, because my grandfather's belt buckle was eye level to me. It was a big silver buckle, much bigger than the size of my hand. It had a gold-plated roadrunner on it and the name Tex etched into it.

The cowboy threw the horses reigns over a rail and walked up to me. He grabbed me with one hand and effortlessly picked me up and held me over his head. He stared at me.

"So, you're my grandchild, then."

"Yes, sir."

"Welcome, then. Everyone calls me Tex."

"Thank you, sir."

"Call me sir again, son, and we're going to have words. My name is Tex."

As he set me down, I saw the gun in his belt.

Tex was declared permanently disabled after World War I. He was gassed and not expected to live long after he came home. But he was too ornery to die. He became a prospector, a rancher, a cattle driver, a surveyor. While the rest of the world "turned civil," he stayed out on the range and lived life his own way.

By the time I knew Tex, he was in his seventies. He died just before he reached one hundred years.

Tex was a storyteller. He remembered things. He remembered every time he was thrown from a horse because of a rattlesnake— "My butt was as black as a blueberry pie." And he always settled scores—he knew how to cook rattlesnake. He remembered finding gold and fighting a shootout with rustlers.

Tex's stories were true for the most part. He lived an incredible life.

I did not see very much of Tex after that first visit. But when he died, my grandmother sent me his belt buckle. I still have it, and I have Tex's tan ten-gallon hat.

And I have memories of a big man full of tales.

Angels in Our Dust

"You and I are going to talk," Mike said in his no-nonsense way as he walked up to me and poked me in the chest.

Mike was a mountain of a man, twenty years my senior but built like a rock. A poke in the chest from Mike was a physically punishing ordeal. No rational person could ever say no to Mike.

I was a young man. I had just been kicked out of the church for which I had been both a youth pastor and a teacher. I was in shock as I saw my chosen vocation unravel in front of me.

I reluctantly got into Mike's dirty white slant six Dodge Dart with cigarette burns and ashes covering the interior. Little did I realize I was about to receive the most genuine and gracious gift I have ever received from the most unlikely of beings.

Mike said, "We're going to talk theology, because your head is all messed up." I agreed with the messed up part but was not certain Mike was the one to undo the damage. He pulled up to the White Spot Tavern and said, "We're going to talk in there."

I tried to resist, saying I did not go into taverns, mumbling that, as a Christian, I did not think it was a very good testimony for me to be in there. But as I said, gainsaying Mike was never productive. So we entered, and I squirmed uncomfortably, watching Mike order a beer and light another cigarette with the smoldering butt that had just left his mouth.

To the back drop of clinking glass, a squeaking jukebox, the crash of pool balls, and the strong odor of smoke and urine, Mike began with something like, "Skeeter, you don't understand the grace of God, because you don't understand yourself." He did not care that I knew all the verses on grace already.

Once, perhaps twice, a week for the next few years, this man took me to this or some other beer dive in town and drilled the facts into my "pretty little head."

Mike did know the facts. His childhood had been spent as the sex pet of his mother and her friends. His huge hands would tremble as he tried to brush away another memory in the middle of a diatribe on the relationship of mercy and grace.

Sometimes his brazen voice would tremble when he admitted he was afraid "his past was the only future he could ever have."

He worshiped women and wanted a wife, but he was afraid of doing violence, so he watched them from a safe distance. He told me in his stuttering way that grace had reached past people far more worthy and come to him.

Mike was broken, but he understood himself.

Mike also knew all the issues. He once introduced me to his storage space, a ten-by-fifteen-foot unit filled with books. The door would hardly close for all the books. And yes, he had read them all, and yes, he knew what they said.

No subject was too obscure for Mike to explore, and no issue was too dangerous for Mike to not give it his full attention.

He gave me some books once, saying I might "need them one day." They included subjects such as terrorism, racist apology, Catholic theology, and esoteric philosophy, and there was a short book on the history of the Baptists.

That was Mike. He told me I have no right to make pejorative comments unless I truly understand those I claim to oppose.

He died a few years ago.

He died a lonely man in Boston, in an apartment a long way from the Georgia hills where I knew him. He died surrounded by beer bottles and cigarette butts.

Why Boston?

Probably because he had not been there before.

Mike's family did not care about his death, but people like me, from all around the country, did. Before the morgue could send his unclaimed body to a science lab, a mutual friend called me and informed me of Mike's death. We called other friends of Mike and pooled our resources together and paid to have Mike's body sent to a place in Georgia that Mike often spoke fondly about.

Over the years I have learned I was not the only person who felt a debt to Mike for offering to us a mirror into ourselves and a window into grace.

Now for me, a beer joint in any town is like a house built for God's kingdom. Each time I frequent such an establishment, I remember Mike, I remember grace, and I wonder if I have yet understood myself the way Mike wanted me to.

ALASKA: NONFICTION

Unalaska

There is an old Alaskan saying: "If you want to know the real Alaska, you have to get off the roads." One place that is certainly off the roads is Unalaska, better known as Dutch Harbor. Unalaska is a place rich in history, both heroic and tragic.

Unalaska's deep natural ports make it strategically valuable for any commercial shipping traversing the Pacific Rim, due to its location some 790 miles down the Alaskan Peninsula on one of the largest of the Aleutian Islands, Unalaska Island.

A place of contrasts, Unalaska is both a safe harbor from the turbulent Pacific Ocean and the frequent target of hurricane level storms. Category three and four storms are so common that the locals treat them with a shrug.

Just getting to Unalaska is an adventure. The thin strip of tarmac at Dutch Harbor's airport, with deep blue ocean water on each end, boasts to be North America's smallest legal commercial jet runway, a fact punctuated by a public road at the north end, which is counted as the runway's last few legal feet. A landing in a small 737-200 jet thrusts passengers forward amidst the screaming of brakes and jet thrusters in full reverse as the craft skids to a stop within a precious few yards of the ocean. To the white-knuckled passengers, Unalaska bids a welcome to the real Alaska.

The treeless landscape of Unalaska Island gives it's emerald texture of shrubs and bristled grass a surreal feel. Wildlife is no bigger than a red fox, though bird life is abundant, making the island a bird watcher's paradise; most noticeable is the stunning population of bald eagles.

For commercial and sports fishing alike, Unalaska has no equal. For than twelve years running, Dutch Harbor produced more commercial tons of fish per year than any other American port. For sports fishing, Halibut top the scale of the variety of world-class catches recorded basis from the returning charter boats full of happy, if perhaps seasick, sports fishing enthusiasts.

Harvesting the sea has defined Unalaska for thousands of

years. Out on the Aleutians, there really is little else to sustain human life. This story of the island and the sea begins with a kind and gentle people called the Unangan, whom the Russians called the Aleuts, for whom the Aleutian Islands are named.

Thousands of years of Aleut fishing skills include the building of the original sea kayaks, which are still looked upon today with great admiration for their seaworthy design. With these vessels, the Aleuts could fish, traverse, and populate the Aleutian Islands and trade as far as South America. Sadly, only a few of the Aleutian Islands remain inhabited today.

The Russians were first to encounter the Aleuts, in recent history, and observed their skill at fishing, the Russians invaded *Ounalashka* to force the Aleuts to fish for Russia. The Aleuts' unsuccessful resistance resulted in their indentured service as fishers for Russia until the Alaskan purchase by the United States.

The United States had other designs on Ounalashka beyond fishing. It saw the island's large natural seaports as an important safe haven in the Pacific. And with the exception that the US military continued to indenture Aleuts to hunt seals for use in manufacturing winter coats as part of their American duty, the Aleuts were otherwise able to regain much of their autonomy after the purchase of Alaska by the United States.

World War II was a tragic time for Ounalashka. The Japanese invaded some of the lower Aleutian Islands, the only US soil ever occupied by a foreign power.

The locals sometimes call this the Other Forgotten War.

The US military chose Ounalashka as the place to establish a base to mount a counterattack against the Japanese invaders. They annexed a small strip of flat land between two hills, with deep water on either side, and installed a runway. They then established a military camp around the runway, and they named this base Dutch Harbor, after the nonindigenous legend of a Dutchman who, it was said, sought harbor there in a storm.

The Aleuts, in an effort to retain their autonomy, quickly incorporated the rest of the island as the township of Unalaska.

It was not long before the Japanese began to bomb Unalaska Island, causing significant damage, though as few as twelve Aleuts died in the raids. After the raids ended, the military imposed a forced evacuation of all Aleuts off the island to internment camps in South Central Alaska. The island dwellers had little warning and were allowed to take nothing with them.

However noble the justification for this evacuation may have sounded, the result is one of the United States' darkest moments.

The conditions in the camps and were so deplorable that more than 50 percent of the Aleuts died of disease and malnutrition. Their misery was only exacerbated when they were finally returned to an island with most homes and property destroyed and the infrastructure gone. Abandoned ammunition and land mines were a constant threat. The cleanup of various defense materials is still going on today.

A Russian Orthodox mission almost single-handedly brought restoration and dignity back to the Unangan people and their island. Today these gentle people seem almost embarrassed at any mention of this travesty, and one would suspect they would never tell the story for themselves.

A small, unpretentious war museum sits next to the airport at Dutch Harbor and is a necessary place to visit on the island. It both tells the tales of the bloody but heroic US victories to recapture the Aleutian Islands and holds few punches in telling the travesty visited upon the country's own protectorate.

Unalaska is a genuine piece of Alaska. It is an adventure from landing to take off. From its unique landscape and bird watching to its fishing and history, much awaits to be appreciated.

In addition to the war museum, one should visit the Aleuts' own museum and culture centers. With their permission, one can wander the hills and see old military sites or visit the memorial park. Before the visit ends, one should consider wandering into a tavern and hearing the yarns of the old salts.

Besides, a tavern visit might be a helpful way to prepare for the flight off the island.

Dusty, Orange Plastic Chairs

My departure from the treeless, windswept island was characteristically delayed, and I needed some relief from the torture of the dusty, orange plastic chairs the designers of the airport terminal in Dutch Harbor, Alaska, maliciously provided. So, it was a combination of boredom and a sore butt that motivated me to visit the tiny WWII museum, a short walk from the airfield.

I enjoy history but usually avoid national war museums because I generally find them to be disingenuous about their nation's role in certain military campaigns.

I offered my four dollars to the lonely employee, who seemed startled by the appearance of a visitor. He was wearing medals from his tour of duty in Vietnam.

Turning back to his book, he pointed to a room to his right. "If nothing else," he said, "look in there."

I followed his single piece of advice.

The room featured only a few artifacts: a kayak, a basket, a hat, and a few fish-bone tools. None of the artifacts appeared to be military.

But on the floor, arranged in white, tombstone-like columns reminiscent of a military burial ground, were freestanding displays, and on them were black and white photos with extensive captions.

The first photo to capture my attention was of a man standing at a harbor watching a departing ship filled with waving passengers. The three-hundred-seventy-person-capacity ship was now laden with five hundred and seventy Aleuts, forced to evacuate their islands under the possible threat of a Japanese invasion.

During the sudden evacuation, the evacuees were stripped of all possessions except one carrying case and the clothing on their backs.

Because the man in the foreground was less than one-eighth Aleut, he was not allowed to board the ship, and he was watching his wife and two children who had been forcefully removed from him sail away.

He would never see them again.

Another photo depicted Funter Bay, an abandoned fishing camp near Juneau, Alaska, which was the internment site for some of the evacuated Aleuts. The internees were disembarked there with few provisions and the soon-to-be broken promise of food and supplies. They faced decaying buildings, no electricity, no source of heat, and a tainted water source located near dilapidated outhouses.

The Aleuts, most of whom had never seen a tree in their lives, suddenly found themselves in damp rain forest conditions with no usable shelter. There was no medical help available, and they soon became victims of pneumonia and tuberculosis.

The captions of more photos described how every tribal elder died in those camps, along with most of the children.

The photos contained many stories. One explained how every female Aleut twelve years of age and older had been stripped naked and examined crudely by doctors. There were photos of another camp where the locals sued to prevent the Aleuts from working or shopping in town. And there were photos of the villages back on the Aleutians. It was US soldiers, not the Japanese, who ransacked Aleut homes, stole religious artifacts from their churches, and razed every building.

The Aleuts eventually returned to barren earth where they once had houses, boats, and fishing gear. What was once home became as hostile and deadly as conditions in the internment camps.

As if to punctuate the travesty, one photo was displayed of another camp, just twenty-two miles from Funter Bay, called Excursion Inlet, which housed about seven hundred Nazi POWs. The Nazi prisoners were given warm clothing, good sleeping conditions, regular meals, and medical care.

There was not a single loss of life from disease in the Nazi prisoner camp.

I left the cenotaphs and paused by the curating soldier bent over his book.

"Can this be true?" I asked.

"That's not the half of it," he said, and his eyes flitted away.

I escaped back to the airport and the relative comfort of the dusty, orange plastic chairs.

Empty Nets

He was a big man with giant hands that greeted mine with a
friendly crush. We were meeting so I could complete a safety
inspection of a fish processing plant located on a remote island in
Alaska. He took me on a tour of the facilities. Enormous post-and-
beam buildings built in 1914 looked as strong and sturdy as the day
they were completed.

With details only a man who had spent a life at the plant could
have known, he explained each piece of machinery, along with the
repair and upkeep information I needed for my reports. He pointed
to the giant wrench built to bring the catch up out of the water
from the commercial fishing boats and the conveyer system
designed to bring the squirming mass of fish past the counting
house and to the processors. He described the mechanics of
processing the waste and returning it to the ocean.

He showed me the newly rebuilt twin diesel engines that
powered the whole operation.

"We're too far away from town to take advantage of local
power," he explained.

He showed me a map of the water system and described how
the original designers of the plant built a water collection system
from the mountain's runoff. He showed me the aqueduct system
that had carried water virtually maintenance-free to the large tank
and purification system for almost a century.

With amazing precision, he explained how the whole process
worked as we walked.

He showed me the original surveyor's map from 1914 and
explained how everything was the same, except one building that
burned down in 1985. We walked along the rows of bunk beds
where the summer help stayed and into the mess hall where the
giant cast iron stove still fully functioned.

He took me to his cottage where he and his wife had raised
two sons—big square, sturdy logs with a bright green metal roof.
His wife stepped out and gave him a big smile and eagerly shook

my hand.

He showed me rows of neatly placed boats in the giant enclosed dry dock and pointed to the gears and ropes that are used by a breed of men who negotiate angry seas for a living.

We walked into the large storage building filled with huge nets neatly piled high, nets staged with anticipation for the next season.

He introduced me to the plant's crew, working as they did every winter to replace long planks of wood suffering from dry rot, update wiring systems, repair motors, overhaul the diesel engines, and paint the iron works and pulleys all around the plant.

As I shook the hands of the crew, I noticed missing fingers and scars that showed these men also once faced the angry seas.

Everything was being put in working order for the next fishing season. A season that would never come.

"Is this hard for you?" I asked. "A life time spent fishing, and suddenly it's over?"

I anticipated affirmation, but I was surprised by the pain I saw in his eyes.

"This is killing me," he said. "It was a wonderful life: hard, dangerous, and often deadly, but everyone loved it." He looked around the plant. "To think that this plant that supported this town for nearly a century is now nothing more than a potential tourist attraction. Our only hope is that the cruise ships will stop here to tour. Last year we were a hardworking, productive, salt-of-the-earth community; this year we are begging for coins from strangers.

"For three months now, the fishermen have been asked to come get their boats, gear, and nets from the warehouse, but they're too discouraged."

"What caused it?" I asked.

"Times have changed, and we haven't."

The halls of the processing plant are being converted into curiosity shops, salmon bakes, and native culture venues. Displayed as if they are artifacts from distant history, rows of boats, pulleys, and empty nets wait in stillborn readiness.

Place of the Winds

The pilot warned of a few bumps on the landing, because "the crosswind can be interesting." The crosswind seemed rather mild to me, but I felt we were approaching the runway far too high. I assumed the small craft was about to fly over and approach the from the other direction. Then I noticed, down on the ground, the wind sock seemed to be pointing stiffly across the runway.

At that moment, we seemed to drop out of the sky.

At the same time a freight train of wind hit us and spun the plane sideways as we fell the remaining few hundred feet.

I was looking out my side window straight down the runway, and just before an all but certain crash landing, the pilot threw the engine into full throttle and turned the nose the right direction just as we hit the icy pavement.

Glancing at me, the pilot said, "You should see it on a windy day."

Knowing he was looking for signs of distress or loss of bodily fluids from a greenhorn, I mustered up a chuckle and spouted something inane and completely off subject.

Everything in Skagway is walking distance from the airport, but the wind was so icy cold that just a few hundred feet was a foreboding task, and I gladly accepted the offer of a ride to the only open motel.

As I walked in, the motel owner looked up at me with surprise and asked how I came to town. I informed her I came in on the mail plane. She gave me a look of respect and said not even the townsfolk fly in the mail plane that time of year.

The owner told me Skagway takes its name from a Tlingit word meaning "place of the north winds." I told her I grew up in a place in Africa called Kijabe, which also means "place of the winds." But the winds "ain't this damn cold in Africa." This impressed her and soon became the talk of the town. Each place I visited already knew the story before I got there, and the story seemed to grow without my help.

In Skagway, my African soul was challenged by a steady thirty-mile-per-hour wind on a—mild—ten-degree day. Townsfolk claimed they don't notice the wind until it gets to at least fifty miles per hour.

Soon my work in Skagway was done, and I had no more time for the tales, coffee, and offers to come back and visit— "Just don't do it in the summer when all the tourists get here," they advised. I smiled that I had somehow managed to avoid the tourist label.

I sat at the little airport, watching for the mail plane to return and fly me to the next town. It was snowing hard, the visibility was low, and I knew I had come in on one of the few flights that had made it to Skagway in weeks.

My only other way out was a ferry that would not be there for another three days—too much time for me to wait if I could help it.

Would the mail plane make it back or was I going to become a temporary resident of Skagway?

But soon enough, the little plane burst out of the sky, preforming its dance with the wind, landed, and skidded up to the building.

The pilot jumped out with a grin and asked me if I was willing to do it all again. He said he had wanted to get his plane to Skagway just to find out if I would be willing to get back in the craft.

"Heck," I said, "I figure if I get killed, you do to."

The pilot laughed and said he wasn't planning on dying that day.

I jumped in the plane, and we were off.

Northern Lights

The jet landed in a billow of snow and drifted to a stop in front of
the small airport. The pilot welcomed us to Kotzebue, announcing
a local temperature of negative thirty-five degrees Fahrenheit. We
began wrestle on our parkas as the flight attendants instructed us to
exit down the ramp and cross the snowy tarmac to the terminal.

I hurried past several hangers to Grant Aviation to make final
arrangements for my last chartered flight to Norvick, a small village
hidden beyond the frozen horizon.

As I stepped into the hanger, I could hear a slight crinkling
sound from my beard. I glanced at my reflection in a window and
saw that in the few-moments' walk to the hanger, my beard had
turned white, and miniature icicles now hung from my mustache.

My pilot stood looking out the window as the wind rocked his
small Cessna on the runway.

I asked if it was still possible to make the prearranged flight.
He shook his head and informed me he could not take the risk.

The trip to the village would be safe enough, he explained, but
after landing, the fuel tends to thicken, and often this will strand
the plane until the temperature moderates. If this happened, we
would likely be stuck in Norvick for a week, because no immediate
break in the weather was predicted.

I asked him if there were any alternatives for me, and he
suggested a water taxi and called one for me.

A water taxi is a drive up the frozen Kotzebue Sound to
remote villages that can only be reached by boat or plane any other
time of the year. No roads, just a wild ride up uncharted frozen
ocean.

Most taxi drivers will not do this, and the ones who are willing
really need the money or are just plain crazy.

Soon a young Kotze arrived in his shiny new Ford Aerostar.
He walked into the hanger and asked with a toothless smile where I
wanted to go. I asked him if there had been any water taxi trips to
Norvick that year. He shook his head.

"Naw, no one to go there this time of the year, 'cept maybe you?"

I hesitated as I looked at that kid eager for an adventure, trying to decide if I wanted to put my life in his hands. Hoping for some assurance, I glanced at the pilot, who shrugged his shoulders and looked away.

The kid said he would charge eighty dollars. He figured the drive was about an hour and a half one way.

And soon we were off down the snow-laden road and heading right for the waterfront. Without slowing down, the kid raced down the bank with a wicked scraping sound on the back end of his van and onto the frozen water.

As we raced across the ocean's surface, we weaved around chunks of ice that jutted up like spikes—the result of breaking ice during the initial freeze. The kid explained tide changes cause the broken chunks and, as soon as we got out far enough from the bank, it would smooth out.

Soon we were on smooth ice.

"Can't go out too far," my comrade informed me. "Ice gets thin." We had about a half-mile wide "safe" zone. Too far out and we end up in the ocean; too close and the ice shards will puncture a tire.

It was eleven in the morning and just beginning to become light out. The sun would be up in an hour, and it would be too dark to travel by three. Our window of opportunity was very small. I figured at best we had a half-hour window to make a mistake, or we would be spending the night somewhere in the middle of the ocean, waiting for next light to find our way home.

The kid pointed to a small hill in the distance of that flat part of the world and told me Norvick was at the base of the hill. With this landmark in mind, I could easily gauge our progress.

Soon we bumped up the bank into Norvick and slid to a stop in front of the tribal house, which was the building I had come to inspect. We stepped into the plank building, and an old man spoke up: "Figured you would not be making this stop." He flashed a toothless grin, and I resisted the urge to ask if he was related to my driver.

"I won't be back this way for a few months," I said in my southern drawl. "Thought I better try to get it done on this trip."

I took notes, asked a few questions, and asked the kid if he was ready to go back.

"S'pect we better, or won't make it before dark. It's a cold night on the water."

As we raced back onto the ocean, I began to search the flat, white horizon for some indication of our destination, but things looked identical to me in all directions.

"How do you know where to go?" I asked.

The kid flashed me a grin and said, "Hope the wind and snow don't hide our tire tracks we made getting here."

After what should have been about halfway back, it was beginning to get dark, the tracks were getting harder to follow, and I could not tell the difference between land and ice. Several times, we lost our tracks and drove in wide circles trying to pick them up again. The cloud cover was thick, and it was hard to get a good idea of our bearings.

Finally, my guide came to a stop and said, "We'll have to wait until it's a little darker and see if we can see any lights from the town. I think we are close."

We sat and waited for the deeper dark, both a threat to our lives and our small ray of hope.

The engine could not be shut off, or it would not restart. At best, it would keep running for three or four more hours before it would run out of gas. Our lives seemed to depend on being close enough to town to see its lights.

We took turns every ten minutes getting out of the van and walking in a circle to scan the horizon for any sign of the town.

We talked of the world, politics, and ice fishing. We did not speak of the weather.

Then, it seemed to hit us both at the same time, like a shot out of the fading horizon. A tiny pinprick of light came piercing into the van and disappeared as quickly as it came.

We both stared in the direction we had seen the flicker, transfixed. We did not speak. With our eyes straining, we waited.

The flicker came again. And soon, another light flickered, and another, and another.

Rachel

We arranged to meet at the boat dock near the Salty Dawg Saloon on the Spit in Homer, Alaska. She was going to give me a ride across Kachemak Bay to the house she and her husband were building on an island near Halibut Cove. In order to help me spot her, she told me she was a snappy dresser and wore a hat with flowers in it. I told her I would be the old, fat guy with a floppy hat and was the antitheses of a snappy dresser.

It amused me to see what an Alaskan woman who lived on an island and used a fishing boat to go to the grocery store called snappy. She wore faded blue jeans and a white blouse and a hat that looked like it was stolen from Minnie Pearl. But despite the outfit, this was a beautiful woman. Her long, red hair set against her bronze complexion was not hard to admire.

As we skipped across the ocean, we found a common sense of humor and soon began to laugh at life and our various miseries in it. As we approached the island with, perhaps, twenty or thirty houses scattered over it, we were hailed from everywhere. We, of course, had to stop and speak to most of the hails as we coursed our way among the docks.

Rachel talked of her husband, a fisherman who was, according to her, a giant of a man and bigger than life. She drilled me on my admitted failures with women and marriage, and her advice proved both humorous and sincere.

After a lengthy inspection of the house, a walk in the woods, and several samplings of Corona, we were off back to Homer.

Slipping our way out of the bay and back onto the open ocean, we were stopped several more times by hailing boaters, and I told Rachel it was clear every man on the island was in love with her. I suggested it was a good thing she was married to such a mountain of a man, because she was the kind of woman men would kill for.

She laughed and with a beaming smile asked if I wanted her to find a place for me on the island as well.

I swallowed my tongue and, smiling also, told her I had enough problems with women as it was.

I was amazed at the calm self-assurance of this person. Somehow, the idea that the whole island was in love with her seemed neither an exaggeration nor overly significant, and her tacit acceptance of my observation somehow did not seem the least conceited. She accepted it as if it were simple fact.

Then she told me it was not just the men of the island who were in love with her.

It seemed that one of the newer arrivals to the island was a woman who had just been divorced, and Rachel decided the divorcee needed a wife as much as her husband did. And she began to tell me of all the benefits of having a good wife and how wonderful it is to be a wife and to have one at the same time.

As I stepped off the boat in Homer and turned to say my farewell, she smiled and said that life is not fair. She had lovers from all sides, and I was without anyone. She asked if I would want her to bring her wife up to Anchorage on occasion to help me out a little, as she was more than willing to share, and her wife would be more than willing too.

I hoped my grin masked the image in my mind of an angry giant fisherman pounding on my door.

From somewhere in the distance I heard myself chuckle and tell her I was going to walk away before she was completely inside my head.

She insisted I should not hook up with anyone until she had talked to them and given me her approval first, and I told her I had decided her secret was she was a snappy dresser and I was going to go right out and buy a hat with flowers in it.

The Great Escape

That week I needed to spend the night in Homer in order to get my jobs done, and I had decided to see how practical camping might be on some of my trips and thought this would be my best chance to give it a try. So, with sleeping bag and pad and my Ford Escape outfitted and ready for the adventure, I paid my six-dollar camping fee and parked in a designated camping area on the beach of the Homer Spit.

A pleasant night of sleep it was too, as I occasionally woke to see the Alaskan sun continue its path along the horizon.

I decided this had been a good idea.

Promptly at six, I woke to my alarm and to see the long Alaskan sunset had blended into sunrise. I got up and got ready to head to the airport for my eight o'clock flight. But easing the Escape into drive, I noticed a slight sound of shifting under the tires. Just to be certain, I hit the four-wheel-drive switch and eased the vehicle forward only to hear the telling sound of my tires spinning.

I stepped out to see my front wheels buried in sand almost down to the hub. I looked around at all the vehicles parked on either side of me with their wheels sitting proudly on top of the sand while my small four-wheel-drive SUV was buried.

With little concern and years of experience of unsticking vehicles in Africa, I patiently dug out my wheels, placed rocks for the wheels to climb out on, and cleared sand from underneath my Escape to avoid becoming high centered.

Climbing confidently back into my vehicle, I eased once again into drive and gently nudged the gas pedal, but the sudden sinking feeling of the front end alerted me that this adventure was long from over.

A half a dozen attempts later, I humbly paid a tow truck driver his fee, and he pulled me out of the sand surrounded by the drawn gaze of dozens of other campers.

I watched as other campers drove their two-wheel-drive vehicles one by one out of their campsites, and I drove my Escape to the airport in whipped silence and just in time for my flight.

California Suntan

I have been cold. Working outside in Delta Junction in negative fifty-five degrees in a thirty-mile-per-hour wind is cold. Even the hardiest Alaskans would agree that is a wee bit nippy. My assignment? It was simple. I was to use my trusty commercial-grade surveyor's wheel to measure and diagram some property buildings, take multiple perspective photos, and send them to my boss who lived in California. Oh, certainly boss! That sounds easy. Only one little problem. The surveyor's wheel is frozen solid, and every time I take the digital camera out of my coat pocket, the batteries go dead before I get the first picture. Thirty-minute job? Yes, sir! You get your California-tanned ass up here and try to take a photo of a building at negative fifty-five in thirty-mile-per hour wind. Just a minute boss—I got another call. Hello. This is who? You want to offer me a job? Doing what? No photos outside at negative fifty-five in thirty-mile-per-hour wind, you say? Well, thank you, ma'am. Let me get warmed up, and by the time I get to Fairbanks, I'll come and see you. By the way, ma'am—pardon me for asking—but you don't happen to have a California suntan on your ass, do you? Great. I'll take the job.

ABOUT THE AUTHOR

Skeeter Wilson was born in Kenya along the edge of the Gikuyu highlands. His graduate work was in historical African fiction and creative writing. He now lives in Auburn Washington with his wife and their two dogs. He gardens, holds writers conferences, runs an indie publishing company, and hosts an annual African feast with fellow Africans and friends. When he finds time, he escapes to his writing nook—nestled in the treehouse in his back yard—and writes.

His works include *Worthless People*, the fictional coming of age story of a young white boy growing up in Africa knowing that one day he will have to leave his home and go to a place called America, and *Crossing Rivers*, the beginning of the historical fiction story of a Gikuyu woman who was born in precolonial Kenya and lived the early days of Colonialism in Kenya.

He and his wife Jacque are managing partners of **Lens&Pens Publications, LLC**, a private publishing company dedicated to publishing for independent authors. Titles published include *Metaphors* by T.L. O'Hara, *Nomi's Hiding Place* by Catherine Palmer, *The Big Conservation Lie* by John Mbaria and Mordecai Ogada, and *The Decline of Spiritual Authority in Gikuyu Traditional Religion* by Dr. Peter Kiarie Njoroge.

www.lensandpenspublications.com